Sunshine

Activity Book 2 Class 4

W0383108

Cornelsen

Contents

Symbols

CD 1.9
listen to the CD · CD 1 track 9

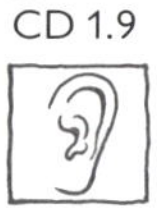
listen

speak

read

play

write

Holidays

CD 1.2

1 **Listen. Number the pictures.**

2 **Where were the children? Read and draw lines.**

holidays in London	holidays in Rome	holidays in Ankara	holidays at home

3 **Write the missing words in the chant.**

She was · I was at home · He was

__________________ in London.

__________________ in Rome.

__________________ in Ankara.

And where were you? I was ____________________________

4 **Where were you in your holidays? Complete the sentence. Draw or glue in a picture.**

I was __________________

____

____

____

Days of the week

1 What day is it? Draw lines.

TU TH SA

MO SU

FR WE

Wednesday

Monday

Sunday

Friday

Thursday

Saturday

Tuesday

2 Number the days in the right order.

Wednesday	Friday	Monday	Thursday	Tuesday	Sunday	Saturday
☐	☐	1	☐	☐	☐	☐

3 Write the missing words.

sorry · time · see you

1 What about playing football on _____________ ?

Sorry, I haven't got _______ on _______________

2 What about watching TV on _____________ ?

OK. ___________________

on ___________________

3 What about meeting friends on __________ ?

________ , I haven't got time on _____________

Wörter lesen und nummerieren (S. 58) · Sätze vervollständigen (S. 60)

1 A trip to London

Going to London

CD 1.8

1 Listen. Number the pictures.

2 Read. Colour the pictures.

Harry is on the red bus. · Kate's dad has got a green car.
The train to London is blue. · The underground is grey.

3 Fill in the missing words. Draw the pictures.

 train	 bus	 car	 car	 bus	
 boat	 train	 bus	 boat	 train	
 taxi	 underground	 bus	 underground	 boat	
 underground	 car	 train	 bus	 taxi	

In London

1 Write the missing words.

2 Read the sentences. Where are they going? Draw lines.

1 Harry, Kate and her dad go to London by  ____________.

2 They go to Buckingham Palace by  ________________.

3 They go to Tower Bridge by  ____________________.

4 They _________ to the London Eye by  ______________.

5 ______________ to London Zoo by  ________________.

boat · bus · taxi · train · underground

3 Colour the words yellow.
Write the missing letters.
Write the missing word in Mr Mole's speech bubble.

I like ____________

F	K	S		O	N	D		N	■	E	Y	E	M	B	S	R
B	U	C	K	I		G	H	A	M	■	P	A	L	A	C	E
A	C	P	L	O	N		O	N	■	Z		O	Y	N	X	M
N	R	I	V	E	R	■	T	H	A	M	E	S	Q	R	U	V
V	R	T	Z	U	B	A	X	B	I	G	■	B	E		K	C

Wörter schreiben (S. 68)

Go to Big Ben

1 Read.

2 Play the game.

- ⚀ Go to the River Thames.
- ⚁ Go to Tower Bridge.
- ⚂ Go to London Zoo.
- ⚃ Go to Big Ben.
- ⚄ Go to the London Eye.
- ⚅ Go to Buckingham Palace.

I was there: ✓

☐ Buckingham Palace ☐ the London Eye ☐ Tower Bridge
☐ London Zoo ☐ the River Thames ☐ Big Ben

3 What time is it? Write the words.

eight · eleven · five · four · nine · one · seven · six · ten · three · twelve · two

(1) 

It's ______________ o'clock.

It's ____________ o'clock. (2)

(3) 

________________ o'clock.

_________________________ (4)

A ticket to London Zoo

1 How much are the boat tickets? Fill in the prices.

2 Talk with a partner.

bus	all sights	£ 1.50
underground	all sights	£ 1.50
boat	London Eye	£
	London Zoo	£
	Tower Bridge	£
	Big Ben	£

Single Travel
Waterloo to London Zoo
on SON 27 AUG 2006
1 CHILD
A TOTAL OF £4.30
WAS PAID BY CASH
THE VALUE OF THIS TICKET
IS £4.30
L1238/00167 (12:13)
ISSUED AT WAT

Single Travel
Waterloo to Tower Bridge
on SAT 26 AUG 2006
1 CHILD
A TOTAL OF £2.50
WAS PAID BY CASH
THE VALUE OF THIS TICKET IS £2.50
L1238/00167 (14:53)
ISSUED AT WATERLOO PIER

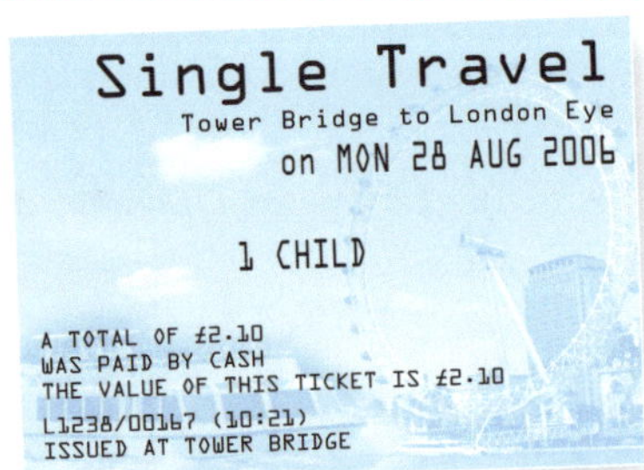
Single Travel
Tower Bridge to London Eye
on MON 28 AUG 2006
1 CHILD
A TOTAL OF £2.10
WAS PAID BY CASH
THE VALUE OF THIS TICKET IS £2.10
L1238/00167 (10:21)
ISSUED AT TOWER BRIDGE

Single Travel
Waterloo to Big Ben
on FRI 24 AUG 2006
1 CHILD
A TOTAL OF £3.60
WAS PAID BY CASH
THE VALUE OF THIS TICKET
IS £3.60
L1238/00167 (12:13)
ISSUED AT WATERLOO PIER

3 Complete the sentences.

____________ : Let's go to ____________________
(Name)
by ____________________

____________ : Great idea!
(Name)

____________ : A ticket to ____________________ , please.
(Name)

____________ : That's ____________________ , please.
(Name)

____________ : Here you are.
(Name)

____________ : And here's your ____________________
(Name)

4 Read the dialogue with your partner or partners.

Portfolio: A postcard from London

1 Write a message on the postcard.

2 Draw or glue a stamp and pictures on the postcard.

Greetings from

LONDON!

Check your English

Ich fand die Aufgabe ☺ leicht 😐 mittel ☹ schwer

1 What time is it?

(Name) ______________________ und ich haben uns gegenseitig gefragt, wie spät es ist. ☐

Diese Zeiten haben wir uns diktiert:

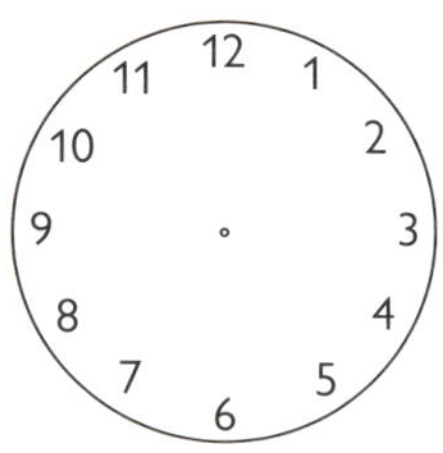
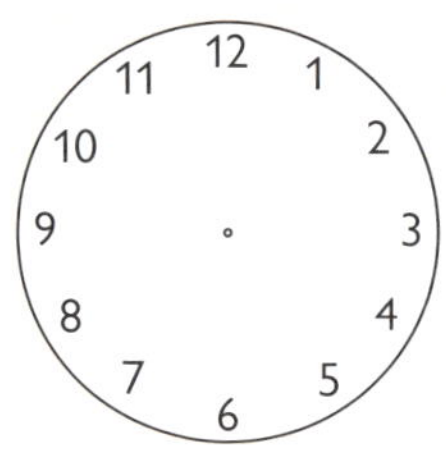
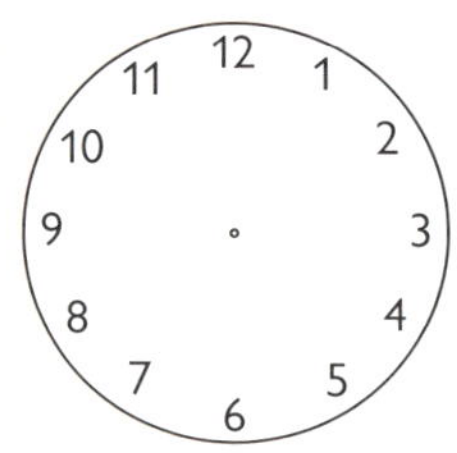
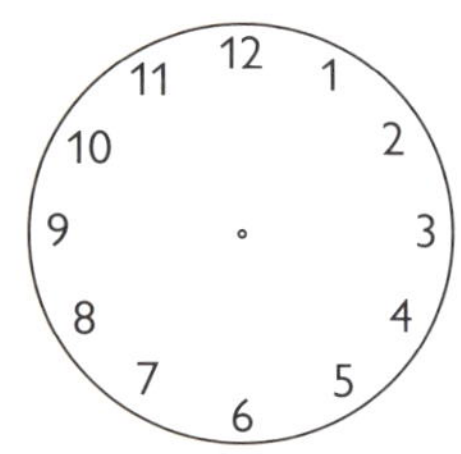

2 Let's go to Big Ben

Ich habe mit (Name) ______________________ das Gespräch geführt. ☐
Wir haben dazu diese Minibildkarten benutzt:

Let's go to:

 ☐
 ☐
 ☐
 ☐
 ☐
 ☐

Let's go by:

 ☐
 ☐
 ☐
 ☐

3 A whale in the River Thames

Ich habe (Name) ___________________ die Geschichte *A whale in the River Thames* vorgelesen. ☐

What's the weather like?

CD 1.15

1 Listen and number the pictures.

2 Write the words.

bus · bike · car · ice cream
jacket · ~~park~~ · shoes · taxi

park ______ ______ ______ ______

______ ______ ______ ______

3 Write the words.
Draw pictures.

What's the weather like?

It's cloudy.
It's foggy.
It's rainy.
It's snowy.
It's sunny.
It's windy.

Monday

Thursday

Friday

Tuesday

The weather

1 Read the temperatures.

2 Write the temperatures. Play Bingo.

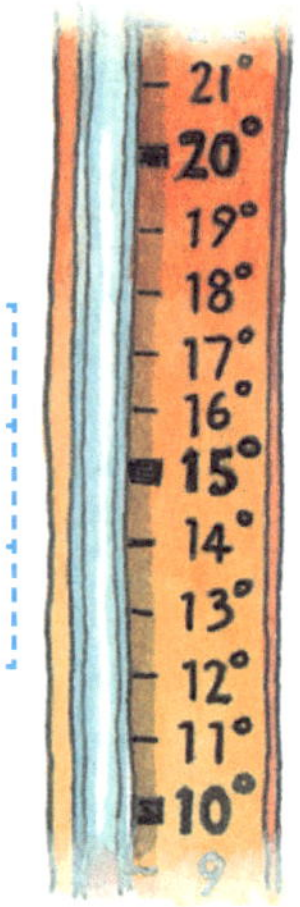

Monday	Tuesday	Wednesday	Thursday	Friday	Saturday	Sunday

3 Talk to a partner: What's the temperature on ...?

4 Read the sentences.

5 Listen. What sentence is missing? Circle the sentence.

CD 1.16

6 Number the sentences. Write your text.

7 Present your text.

- [ ] Today is Wednesday.
- [ ] Have a nice day.
- [ ] I'm Ted Miller.
- [ ] Here's the weather.
- [ ] Good morning.
- [1] This is BBC 1.
- [ ] It's sunny today.
- [ ] It's 18°.

This is ______________________________

____

____

____

____

Zahlen im Spiel festigen (S. 85) · Sätze lesen, in die richtige Reihenfolge bringen, (ab-)schreiben und präsentieren (S. 87)

Seasons

1 Read the months.

2 Write the months.

April · August · ~~December~~ · February
~~January~~ · July · June · March · May
November · October · September

Winter

Spring

Summer

Autumn

Winter	Spring	Summer	Autumn
December			
January			

3 Listen. Draw lines from number to number.

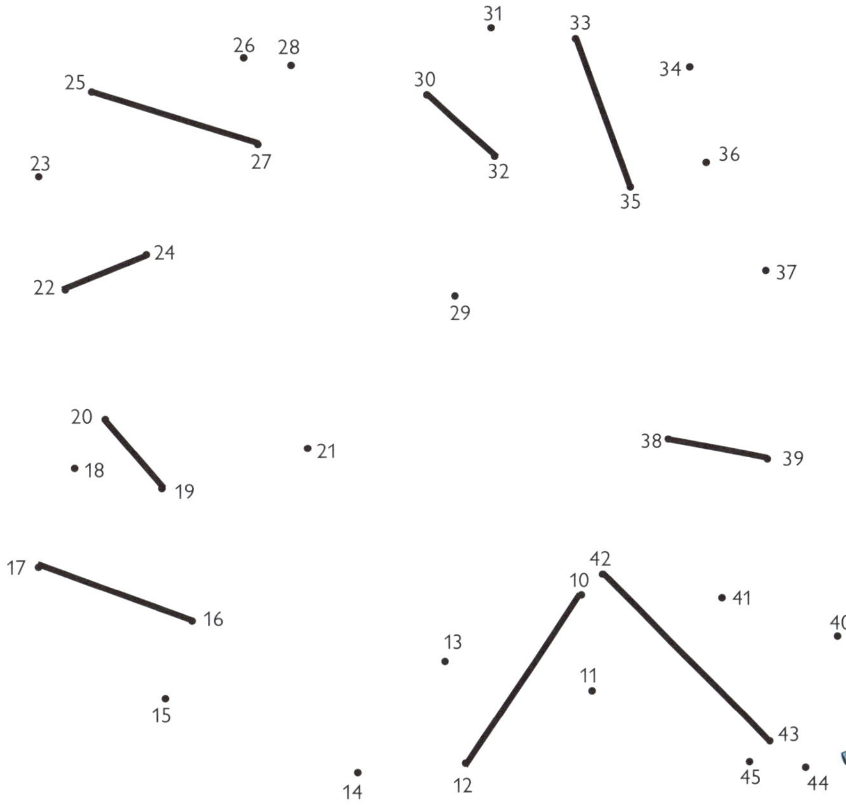

Game of the year

1 Read the sentences.

←(1)	Go back 1.	(3)→	Go forward 3.
	Throw again.		Miss a turn.

2 Make your own rules.

2	A snowy Saturday in January.	(2)→
5	Snowdrops in winter.	
7	A birthday in March.	
9	Daffodils in spring.	
11	25° on Sunday.	
12	A rainy Monday in June.	←(2)
14	A cold Tuesday in summer.	
17	Red roses in July.	
19	Summer holidays.	
20	A sunny Wednesday in August.	
22	A cloudy Friday in September.	
23	A windy Thursday in October.	
24	Spiders in autumn.	
27	A foggy Monday in November.	
29	15° on Christmas Day.	

Portfolio: My birthday month

1 **Write the month and number the days in your calendar.**

____

MO	TU	WE	TH	FR	SA	SU

2 **Complete the sentences.**

My name is _______________________________

My birthday is _______________________________

_______________ is in _______________

The weather in _______________ :

____

3 **Draw or glue things from your birthday month.**

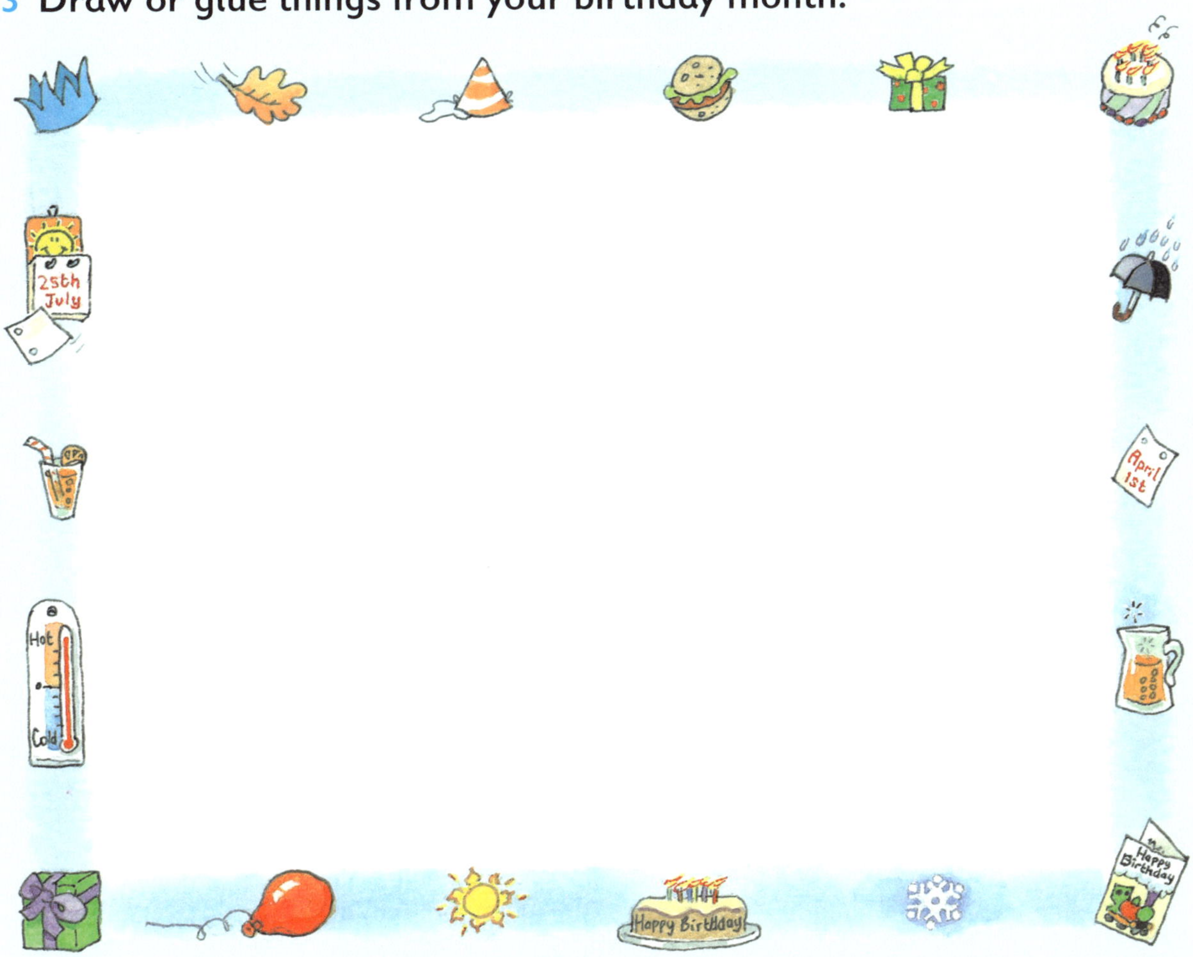

Check your English

Ich fand die Aufgabe ☺ leicht ☹ mittel ☹ schwer

1 Chant: Snowdrops in winter

Ich habe (Name) ____________________ den *chant*

Snowdrops in winter vorgelesen. ☐

 *in winter.*  *in spring.*  *in summer.*

What will autumn bring?

Ich habe den *chant* auswendig aufgesagt. ☐

2 What's the weather like?

Monday	Tuesday	Wednesday	Thursday	Friday	Saturday	Sunday

(Name) ____________________ und ich haben uns gegenseitig das Wetter an verschiedenen Wochentagen diktiert. ☐

3 A weather report

Ich habe (Name) ____________________ einen Wetterbericht vorgetragen. ☐

(Name) ____________________ hat mir einen Wetterbericht vorgetragen: ☐

☐ Monday ☐ Tuesday ☐ Wednesday ☐ Thursday

☐ Friday ☐ Saturday ☐ Sunday

☐ cloudy ☐ sunny ☐ windy ☐ snowy

☐ foggy ☐ rainy Temperature: ___°

3 At the museum

Animals

1 **Find the animals. How many are there? Write the numbers.**

2 **Write the words.**

crocodile · dinosaur · elephant · lion · monkey · parrot · whale

Where are the animals?

CD 1.21

1 Listen. Where are the animals? Write the room numbers.

2 Look at exercise number one. Complete the sentences.

1 
Excuse me, please. Where are the ________________?

They're upstairs, in room 31.

2 
Excuse me, please. Where are the ________________?

They're downstairs, in room 15.

3 
Excuse me, please. Where are the lions?

They're ____________________, in room _____.

4 
Excuse me, please. Where are the ____________________?

They're __________________, in room _____.

Einen Hörtext verstehen (S. 103) · Informationen aus Abbildungen und Texten entnehmen, Sätze vervollständigen (S. 104)

Talking about animals

1 What animal is it?

2 Which parts of the animals are in the pictures? Write the numbers.

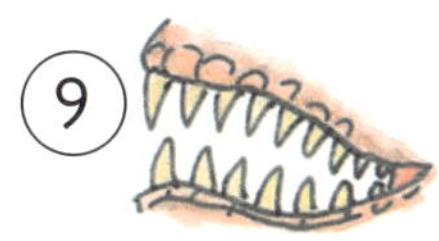

	nose	leg	feet	tail	teeth	arm	ear
parrot							
crocodile							
dinosaur							
elephant							
lion							
monkey							
whale							

3 Where do the animals live? Tick.

	right	wrong
1 Monkeys live in the sea.		
2 Parrots live in rivers.		
3 Elephants live in the jungle.		
4 Crocodiles live in trees.		
5 Lions live in the bush.		
6 Whales live in rivers.		

Wishes

1 Write the missing words.

a monkey's · a whale's · an elephant's
strong tail · big ears · long arms

1 I wish I had ____________________ ____________________

2 I wish I had ____________________ ____________________

3 I wish I had ____________________ ____________________

And you?

4 I wish I had ____________________ ____________________

2 Fill in the names of the animals in your museum. Find out where the animals are in your partner's museum. Write your partner's name and the words.

bird · crocodile · dinosaur · elephant · lion · monkey · whale

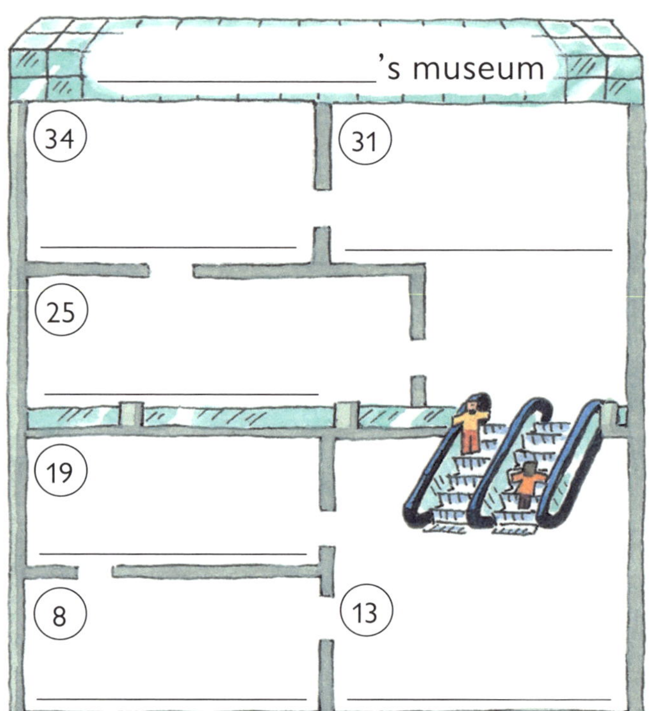

Portfolio: Animal presentation

1 **Glue or draw a picture of your animal.**

2 **Write about your animal.**

3 **Present your text.**

I want to speak about

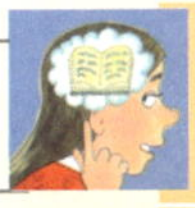

Know your text.

Speak loudly.

Look at the class.

Show pictures.

Check your English

Ich fand die Aufgabe ☺ leicht 😐 mittel ☹ schwer

1 Rhyme: The elephant

CD 1.22

Ich habe den Reim auf der CD angehört. ☐

Ich habe (Name) ____________________ den Reim vorgelesen und ihn auswendig aufgesagt. ☐

2 Where are the lions?

(Name) ____________________ und ich haben uns gegenseitig gefragt, wo die Tiere in unseren Museen ausgestellt sind. Wir haben die Tiernamen in die Räume geschrieben und geprüft, ob wir sie richtig eingetragen haben (Seite 20). ☐

3 Talking about animals

Ich habe (Name) ____________________ meine Tier-Portfolioseite präsentiert (Seite 21). ☐

Ich habe mir den Vortrag von (Name) ____________________ über (Tier) ____________________ angehört. ☐

Folgende Körperteile des Tieres wurden beschrieben:

arms ☐ legs ☐ feet ☐ ears ☐ nose ☐ teeth ☐ tail ☐

4 Keeping fit

Clubs

CD 1.28

1 Where do the children want to go? Draw lines.

2 Make a poster for a club.

Parts of the body

1 Write the words.

arm · ear · eye
foot · hand
head · knee · leg
nose · shoulder
teeth · toe

2 Tick the right parts of the body.

CD 1.30

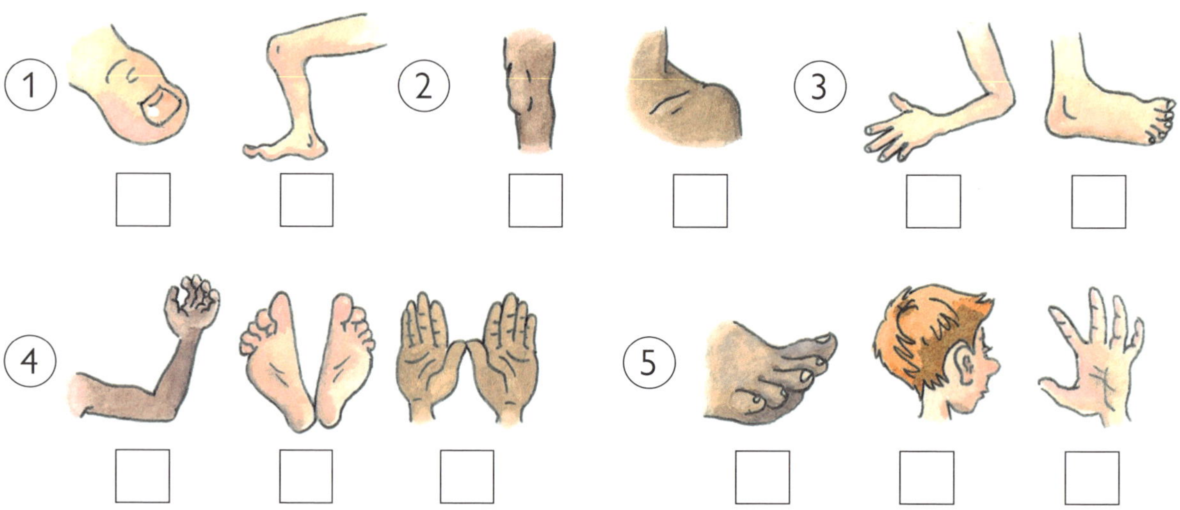

Wörter schreiben (S. 120) · einen Hörtext verstehen (S. 121)

Fitness

1 Complete the sentences.

bend · hop · put · stretch · touch
arms · hands · knees · leg · shoulders · toes

1

2

3

1 __________ your __________

2 __________ on one __________

3 __________ your __________

4 __________ your __________

5 __________ your __________ on your __________

4

5

2 Write a new exercise.

1 ______________________________

2 ______________________________

3 ______________________________

4 ______________________________

5 ______________________________

Activities

1 What can or can't they do? Complete the sentences.

dance · do judo · play table tennis · ride a horse · ski · swim

1

Kate can ______________

2

Emily can't

____

3

Samir ______________________

4

Harry ________________________________

2 What can the children in your class do? Write sentences.

______________________ can ________________________________

______________________ can ________________________________

____

3 Complete the sentences.

bend my knees · play a computer game · stretch my arms · watch TV

1

I've got to

____

____

____

2

I can't

____

____

3

I can't

____

____

4

I've got to

____

____

Sätze vervollständigen und schreiben (S. 126) · Sätze vervollständigen (S. 129)

Portfolio: Sports

1 Write.

I can ______________________________

I can't ______________________________

____

____

____

____

2 What can you do best? Draw a picture.

I can ______________________________ best.

3 Write about your family and friends.

My ______________________________

My ______________________________

My ______________________________

My ______________________________

Check your English

Ich fand die Aufgabe ☺ leicht 😐 mittel ☹ schwer

1 Rhyme: Animal moves

Ich habe (Name) ____________________ den Reim vorgetragen. ☐

2 Can you dance?

(Name) ______________________________ und ich haben uns gegenseitig gefragt, welche Sportarten wir können. ☐

(Name) ______________________________ can:

☐ dance ☐ do judo

☐ play table tennis ☐ ride a horse

☐ ski ☐ swim

3 Sport

Ich habe (Name) ________________ erzählt, welche Sportarten ich kann und welche ich nicht kann (Seite 27). ☐

5 Emails from the USA

I want an e-pal

1 Read the sentences.

2 Listen. Fill in the numbers.

CD 2.2

☐ I'm from Great Britain.

☐ Mole5.

☐ I'm eleven.

☐ It's sunny.

☐ In May.

☐ I've got two rabbits.

☐ Thomas.

☐ My nickname is Tom.

3 Write the answers.

What's your name?

How old are you?

When's your birthday?

Where are you from?

What's your nickname?

What's your password?

Password Superman

Password 3859

Password monster

Sätze lesen und einen Hörtext verstehen (S. 136)
eine Anmeldekarte ausfüllen (S. 136)

Family and jobs

I'm from Great Britain. I live in London.

1 Write.

2 Read to a partner.

____

the USA. ______________

in New York.

And you?

____

____

____

3 Read the sentences to a partner.

4 Write the words.

My father is a mechanic.
My grandmother was a shop assistant.
My sister is a teacher.
My grandfather was a police officer.
My brother is a taxi driver.
My mother is a hairdresser.

I'm a mole and I live in a hole!

Schreiben, wo man herkommt und wo man lebt (S. 138)
Sätze lesen, ein Worträtsel ausfüllen (S. 140)

Jobs and email

1 Write the words.

hairdresser
mechanic
police officer
shop assistant
teacher
taxi driver

2 Read the words and the email.

3 Write the missing words in the email.

my mother · playing with my friends · a small house
eleven · in May · a bus driver · a dog

Hi Harry,

I'm ____________ . My birthday is __________________ . I live with

_______________________ and two sisters. My mother is _________

____________. We have got ______________________ with a garden.

I've got ________________. His name is Rex. I like playing with Rex.

My hobbies are ___________________________________ and writing

emails. What are your hobbies? And what about your family?

Your friend,
Tim

A day in New York

CD 2.7

1 Where does the bus stop? Listen and number.

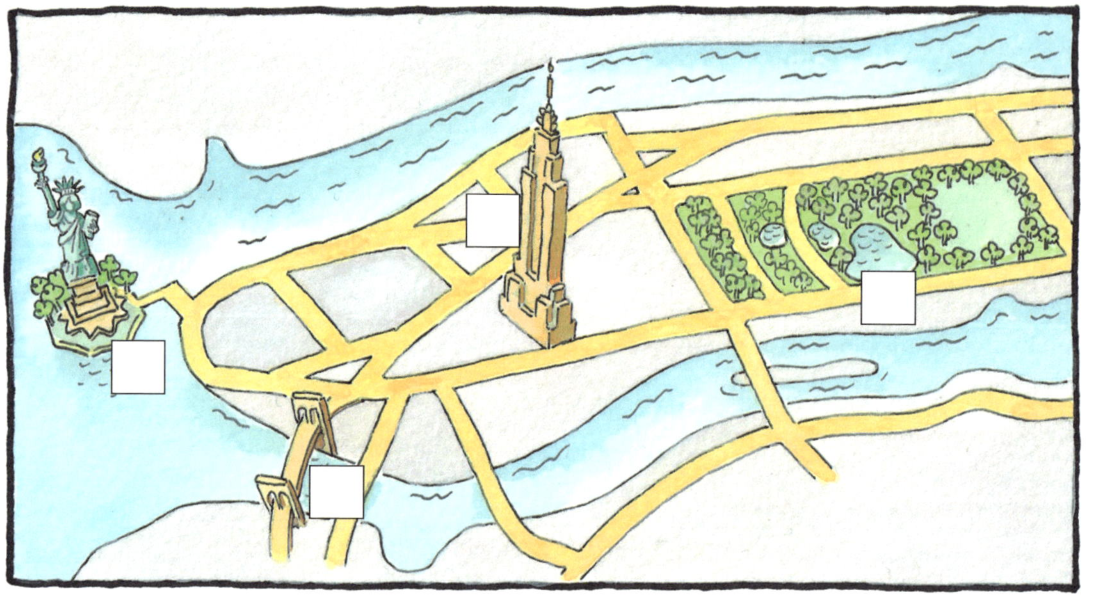

2 What does the police officer ask? Ask a partner. Write the answers.

Name: ______________________

City: ______________________

Street: ______________________

Phone number: ______________________

Mother's name: ______________________

Father's name: ______________________

Einen Hörtext verstehen (S. 148)
Angaben zur Person erfragen und aufschreiben (S. 148)

Portfolio: An email to an e-pal

1 Write an email to an e-pal.

About me

To: ______________________________

Subject: About me

Dear ______________________________

____

____

____

____

____

____

____

____

____

____

____

____

____

____

Eine E-Mail schreiben (S. 145)

Check your English

Ich fand die Aufgabe ☺ leicht 😐 mittel ☹ schwer

1 Where do you live?

Ich habe (Name) ______________________ gesagt, wo ich wohne.

Ich habe nach seiner / ihrer Adresse gefragt. ☐

2 Matt's family

Ich habe (Name) ______________________ Matts Familienmitglieder vorgestellt und gesagt, welche Berufe seine Mutter, sein Vater und sein Bruder ausüben. ☐

Ich habe gesagt, was meine Eltern beruflich machen. ☐

3 My email

Ich habe (Name) ______________________ meine E-Mail auf Seite 33 im Activity Book vorgelesen. ☐

(Name) ________________ hat mir seine / ihre E-Mail vorgelesen.

Sie/Er hat sie an (Name) ______________________ geschrieben.

In the classroom

1 **Which words are on the board? Write.**

2 **Ask a partner what's in the classroom. Tick the words.**

- [x] pupil
- [ ] ______________
- [ ] ______________
- [ ] ______________
- [ ] ______________
- [ ] ______________
- [ ] ______________
- [ ] ______________

3 **Fill in the missing words.**

4 **Read the text with a partner.**

children · good morning
ill · teacher · the day
the weather

Pupil: The ____________ is coming.

Teacher: Good morning, ____________.

Pupil: ____________________, Mrs Brown.

Teacher: Please write ____________ on the board.

Pupil: Today is ____________.

Teacher: What's ____________________ like?

Pupil: It's ____________________.

Teacher: Where's Sally?

Pupil: She's ______, Mrs Brown.

Monday · Tuesday
Wednesday · Thursday
Friday

cloudy · cold · foggy
rainy · snowy · sunny
warm · windy

Wörter erkennen und schreiben, ein Bild besprechen (S. 153)
einen Lückentext ausfüllen und lesen (S. 156)

Rhymes and chants

1 Which sentences go with the pictures?
Colour the boxes the same colour as the picture frame.

2 Number the blue, red and green sentences.

- [ ] She was in Rome.
- [ ] And goodness gracious, What a nose!
- [ ] Daffodils in spring.
- [ ] And where were you?
- [ ] Roses in summer.
- [1] The elephant goes Like this, like that

- [ ] Snowdrops in winter.
- [ ] I was in London.
- [ ] He has no fingers, He has big toes.
- [ ] He was in Ankara.
- [ ] What will autumn bring?
- [ ] I was at home.
- [ ] He's terribly big, And he's terribly fat.

3 Write the rhyme or chant you like best.

4 Read the rhyme or chant to a partner.

____

____

____

____

____

 Zusammengehörende Teile eines Reims finden, einen Reim abschreiben (S. 158)

What do you know about London?

1 Read the words and sentences in the box.

2 Listen. Draw lines between the sights and the speakers.

CD 2.15

3 Write the missing words and sentences.

4 Read with partners.

I don't know the word.
This is London Zoo.
This is Big Ben.
This is Tower Bridge.
Here's the River Thames.
That was bad. · London
Here's the London Eye.

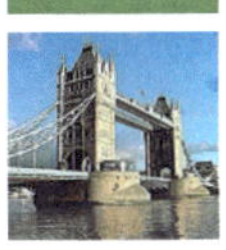

Inspector: What do you know about ______________?

Pupil 1: ______________________________

Pupil 2: ______________________________

Pupil 3: ______________________________

Pupil 4: ______________________________

Pupil 5: ______________________ and this

is … ______________________________

Inspector: Buckingham Palace. ______________

5 Which word doesn't fit? Circle and write the word.

river	(bike)	boat	bridge	bike
sister	teacher	pupil	school inspector	______
crocodile	lion	monkey	hamster	______
lunch box	pencil	ruler	rubber	______
winter	summer	May	spring	______
windy	sunny	rainy	happy	______
angry	late	happy	scared	______

Do you know the words?

1 Find the words and mark them.

2 Write the words under the pictures.

G	U	I	N	E	A		P	I	G
P	E	N	M	S	T	R	A	I	N
H	A	R	R	Y	H	O	N	E	Y
F	O	O	T	B	A	L	L	I	S
B	I	K	E	T	H	E	R	A	T
S	C	H	O	O	L	T	A	X	I
L	I	N	S	P	E	C	T	O	R

3 There are 6 more words. Write the sentence.

4 Tick the right word.

(1) 
☐ happy
☐ angry

(3) 
☐ scared
☐ strong

(2) 
☐ bad
☐ good

(4) 
☐ nice
☐ loud

Wörter im Rätsel finden und aufschreiben (S. 163)
Adjektive lesen und Bildern zuordnen (S. 163)

Portfolio: A school play

1 This was the name of our school play:

____

2 It was on ______________________________________

3 This was our play:

Scene 1 ______________________________________

Scene 2 ______________________________________

Scene 3 ______________________________________

Scene 4 ______________________________________

Scene 5 ______________________________________

Scene 6 ______________________________________

Scene 7 ______________________________________

Scene 8 ______________________________________

6 A school play

4 I was ____________________

5 My friend ____________________ was ____________________

6 My favourite scene was ____________________

Bonfire Night

1 Play with a partner.

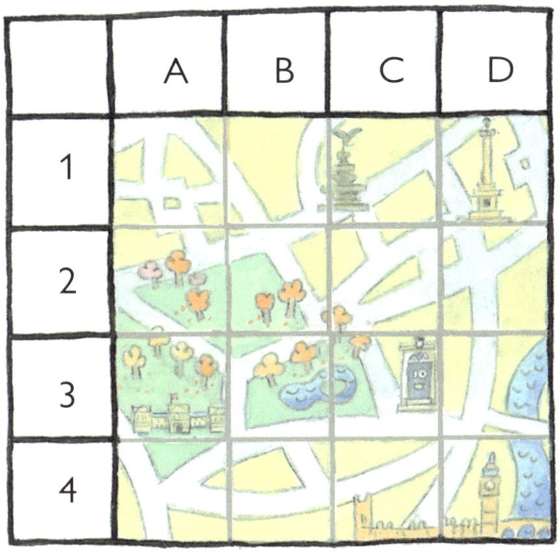

London map A

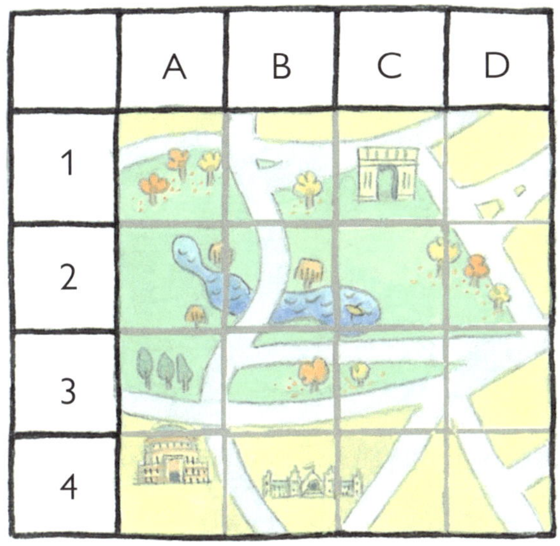

London map B

2 Talk about the pictures.

CD 2.23

3 Listen. Draw lines from the children to their guys.

Christmas

1 What's wrong? Find six mistakes.

2 Complete the sentences.

25 · candy canes · mistletoe · Santa Claus · song · stockings

1 In the USA, Christmas is on ______________ December.

2 ______________________ has got red and white clothes.

3 ____________________________ is green.

4 You can hang _________________________ on the Christmas tree.

5 *Santa Claus is coming* is a Christmas _______________

6 Children in England and the USA hang up

_____________________________ for Christmas.

Über ein Bild sprechen (S. 176) · Sätze vervollständigen (S. 176)

Christmas

CD 2.28

1 Listen. Draw lines.

2 What are their Christmas presents? Write the words.

a bike · a book · a Game Boy · in-line skates · a pullover · a T-shirt

Kate	Mum	Dad
______	______	______
______	______	______
______	______	______

Valentine's Day

1 Write the words.

cards · chocolate · February · flowers · friends · heart
present · red · secret · Valentine

across

2 

3 

4 

8 

9 

down

1 

3 

5 

6 

7 

2 Mr Mole's secret message

What is Mr Mole saying? Each number is a letter (1=A, 5=E, 14=N …).

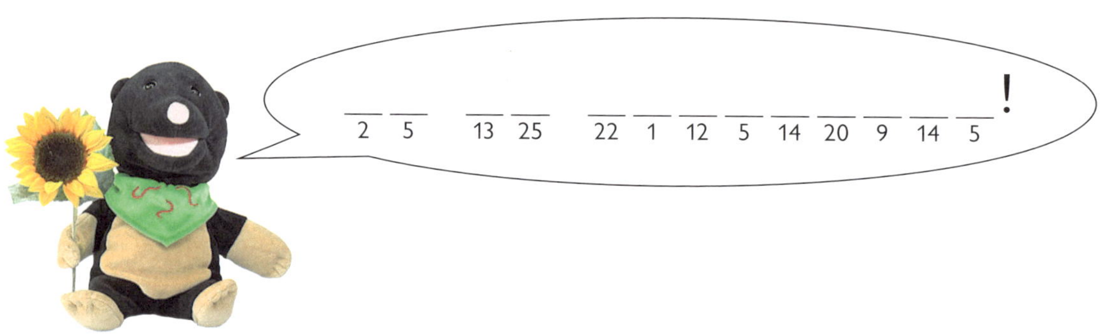

Rätsel lösen (S. 182)

Saint Patrick's Day

1 Colour the rainbow.

2 Draw six snakes.

There's a snake
1 under the tree.
2 on the house.
3 behind the bush.
4 under the dog.
5 behind Saint Patrick.
6 in the grass.

Saint Patrick's Day

1 Find eleven green things. Cross out the words.

apple · banana · boat · bottle · ~~bush~~ · car · dog · grass · happy
ice cream · leprechaun · lettuce · mountain bike · pullover · rainbow
schoolbag · shamrock · shirt · socks · tree

2 Circle eight words. Write the words next to the pictures.

S	H	A	M	R	O	C	K	P	X	L
N	B	R	D	T	H	Y	J	F	D	E
A	V	E	U	I	S	G	C	U	L	P
K	Q	L	F	R	W	I	M	E	V	R
E	X	G	R	E	E	N	H	J	G	E
P	G	M	D	L	X	C	Q	N	K	C
A	C	O	T	A	S	M	A	R	C	H
O	K	G	L	N	Y	B	I	W	E	A
D	Z	N	F	D	R	Z	O	B	P	U
R	A	I	N	B	O	W	A	F	J	N

1  ______

2  ______

3  ______

4  ______

5  ______

6  ______

7  ______

8  ______

Word fields

Days of the week

Transport

London sights

Weather

Wild animals

Body

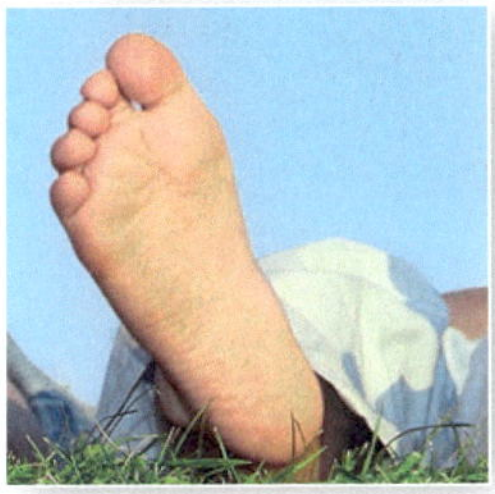

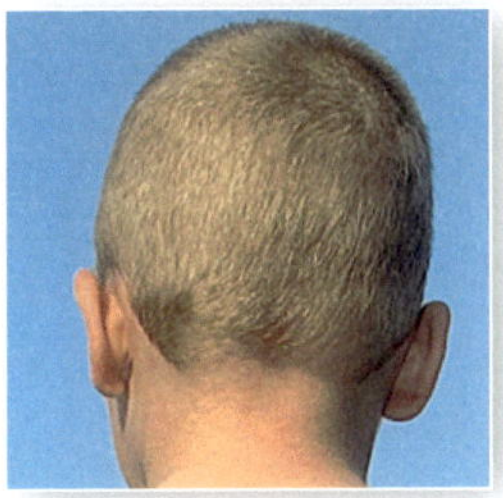

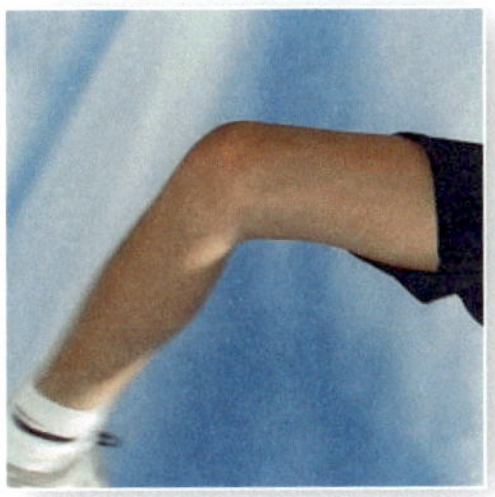

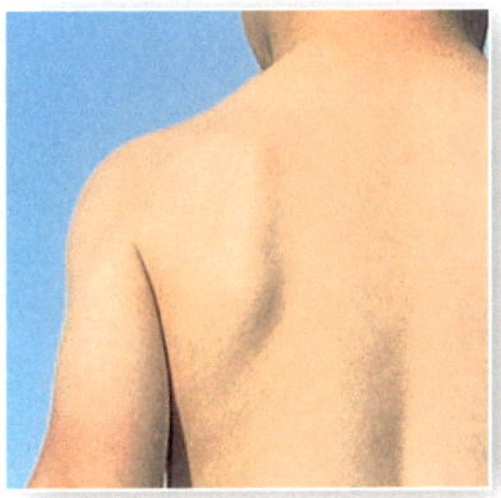

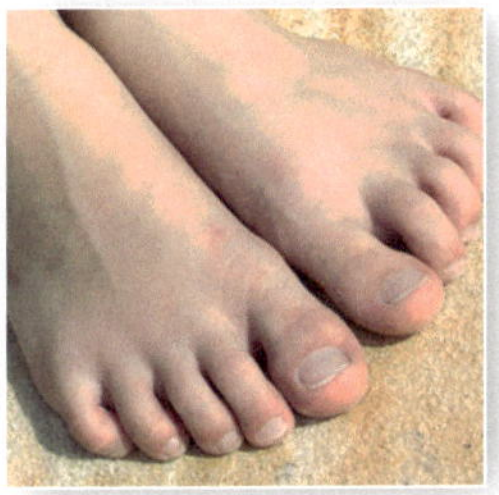

Sport

Jobs

Dear ____________________,

Please come to our play:

____

When

On ____________________

at ____________________

Where

____

From,

____

A school play

Eine Einladung schreiben (S. 163)

Cut-out page

1
Guy Fawkes
This book belongs to:
2
London, autumn 1605
Let's kill the king
3
Yes, let's kill the king with gunpowder.
4
...33... 34...35...36. OK. Let's go.
5
Look at the gunpowder! It's a plot!
6
That's treason!
7
Penny for the guy!
8
Remember, remember
The fifth of November
Gunpowder, treason and plot.
I see no reason
Why gunpowder treason
Should ever be forgot.

Cut-out page

Valentine! · my · Dear · Be · Love,

Roses are red.
Violets are blue
I'm your secret Valentine.
Can you guess who?

Today I am your Valentine
And here is my secret for you:
You are the sweetest girl/boy I know.
I L-O-V-E Y-O-U!